INSPIRING FOOTBALL STORIES FOR KIDS

INSPIRING FOOTBALL STORIES FOR KIDS

15 Amazing Tales of Football Legends – Fostering Resilience, Leadership, and Passion for the Game in Young Champions

BRENDAN STERLING

TABLE OF CONTENTS

INTRODUCTION

Welcome to "Amazing Football Stories for Kids," where every kick, goal, and cheer leaps off the page, inviting you into a world where football isn't just a game — it's a journey of dreams, courage, and friendship. Picture yourself racing down the pitch, the ball at your feet, and thousands of fans chanting your name. Now, what if I told you that within these pages lies the map to turning those dreams into reality?

Clearly, football holds a special place in your heart, but perhaps there are days when the ball just won't cooperate, or you feel like you're not quite part of the team. Don't worry, you're not alone. Every football legend started somewhere, facing challenges and learning to overcome them with perseverance and dedication. This book is your all-access pass to the secrets behind their success, offering you the tools to tackle your own challenges.

Through 15 action-packed stories about football heroes, this book will teach you more than just the history of the sport; it will show you how to develop resilience, find motivation, and discover a sense of belonging that only a team can provide. By the end, you'll be inspired to become the best version of yourself, both on the pitch and in life.

We'll kick off with Lionel Messi's incredible journey from being a young boy in Argentina with big dreams to becoming one of the greatest football players the world has ever seen. His story, like all the others in this book, is a testament to the power of dreams, hard work, and the magic of football. Let's play, and who knows, the next amazing football story could be yours.

LIONEL MESSI – RESILIENT PATH TO GLORY

"It does not matter if I fail, it matters that I do not give up."

- Lionel Messi

EARLY LIFE AND THE BIRTH OF A DREAM

Lionel Messi was born into a family where football was more than just a game; it was a way of life. His father worked at a steel factory in Rosario, Argentina, during the day and coached a local football team by night, while his mother supported the family as a cleaner. From the moment Lionel could walk, he was kicking a football, his tiny feet already showing the signs of future greatness. The Messi family, though not wealthy in material terms, was rich in love, support, and a shared passion for football.

At the tender age of five, Lionel joined his first football team, Grandoli, where his father was the coach. Despite his small stature, he played with a fearlessness and determination that set him apart from his peers. His natural talent was undeniable, but it was his work ethic and dedication that truly made him stand out. Lionel would spend hours practising after school, honing his skills, and dreaming of one day playing professional football.

However, Lionel's journey was not without its challenges. At the age of 11, he was diagnosed with a growth hormone deficiency, a condition that threatened to derail his dreams of becoming a professional football player. The treatment was expensive, and the Messi family struggled to afford the costs. But they never lost hope, and neither did Lionel. He continued to play, to dream, and to work towards his goal, undeterred by the obstacles in his path.

Lionel's talent did not go unnoticed. He quickly rose through the ranks of local youth teams, leaving a trail of awestruck opponents and spectators in his wake. His performances for Newell's Old Boys, a renowned youth club in Rosario, attracted the attention of scouts from around the world. Yet, it was FC Barcelona that saw the potential in Lionel, a potential that went beyond his physical limitations. Not only did FC Barcelona provide an opportunity for him to join one of the world's most prestigious football academies, La Masia, but they also included a commitment to cover the costs of his medical treatment. The offer from Barcelona was a lifeline for Lionel and his family, but the decision to move to Spain was not an easy one. It meant leaving behind his family, friends, and the life he. But Lionel's dream was calling, and it was a call he could not ignore.

FROM BARCELONA TO MIAMI

Under the tutelage of some of the game's greatest minds, Lionel quickly transitioned from a promising talent at La Masia to a cornerstone of Barcelona's first team. At Barcelona, Messi found more than just a team; he found a family and a home. Alongside legends like Xavi, Iniesta, and Puyol, he was part of an era-defining squad that captured hearts and trophies with equal fervour.

Barcelona became synonymous with Messi, and Messi with Barcelona. Together, they reached the pinnacle of club football, claiming numerous La Liga titles, Copa del Rey trophies, and Champions League victories. Messi's impact was monumental, breaking records with a relentless consistency that left the world in awe. He became Barcelona's all-time leading scorer, a testament to his incredible dedication to the club that had given him a chance when he was just a boy with a dream.

The announcement that Lionel Messi was leaving Barcelona in the summer of 2021 marked a poignant turning point in his career. This departure not only stunned the world of football but also ended a chapter that had brought immense joy to Barca fans worldwide. Messi's move to Paris Saint-Germain (PSG) signified the beginning of a new era, where he brought his unmatched talent and passion for football to a new stage, embracing the challenges and opportunities that awaited in Paris. His journey with PSG was watched closely by fans eager to see how the legend would continue to weave his magic in a different league.

In the summer of 2023, Messi's career took another exciting turn as he joined Inter Miami, signalling not just another transfer but a transformative moment for football in the United States. This move to a club teeming with ambition and vibrancy provided Messi with a unique opportunity to further his legacy in a league that is rapidly growing in popularity. Inter Miami, co-owned by football luminary David Beckham, aimed high, seeking to blend the allure of Miami with the passion of football, a goal that resonated with Messi's exceptional standards of excellence.

ARGENTINE PROMISE TO WORLD CUP TRIUMPH

Adorned in the celestial blue and white, Messi's journey with the Argentine national team encapsulates more than a decade of electrifying triumphs and soul-stirring defeats, culminating in a crowning moment that forever immortalised his name in football lore.

From the outset, Messi's path with Argentina was marked by the promise of a prodigious talent, one heralded to return World Cup glory to his nation. His early achievements, including victory at the U-20 World Cup and Olympic gold in Beijing, set high expectations. However, the journey was fraught with significant setbacks. The Copa America and World Cup stages, in particular, tested Messi's mettle. Heartbreaking losses in the 2014 World Cup final against Germany and consecutive Copa America finals against Chile in 2015 and 2016 painted a narrative of unfulfilled potential, casting a shadow over Messi's international legacy. These defeats were not just losses on the scoreboard but profound challenges to Messi's resolve and his enduring bond with Argentina.

Yet, Messi's story is one of resilience. Despite facing criticism and shouldering the immense pressure of a nation's hopes, his dedication never wavered. The 2021 Copa America victory and the triumphant 2022 World Cup campaign in Qatar were testaments to his perseverance. These victories, especially the World Cup win, were redemption, affirming Messi's status as a legend. Messi's legacy with Argentina is a powerful reminder that true champions are forged in the crucible of adversity, embodying the spirit of resilience, passion, and an unwavering commitment to their cause.

OVERCOMING ADVERSITY ON THE FIELD

Throughout his illustrious career, Lionel Messi has not only dazzled the world with his extraordinary talent but also demonstrated an unparalleled resilience in the face of adversity. His journey from a young talent battling significant injuries, including a career-threatening muscle tear in the 2006-2007 season, to becoming one of Barcelona's pivotal figures is a testament to his indomitable spirit.

Messi's resilience reached a climax following a painful arm fracture in the 2017-2018 season, which tested his mental fortitude and physical readiness. His early return and subsequent performances not only highlighted his dedication to football but also served as an inspiration to fans and aspiring athletes worldwide.

Each comeback, marked by spectacular performances, illustrates Messi's ability to overcome physical setbacks and mental battles, showcasing his commitment to excellence and his unbreakable spirit.

THE POWER OF PERSEVERANCE

Lionel Messi's journey, from his modest beginnings in Rosario to his legendary status in football, embodies the essence of never giving up and the power of dreams. Throughout his career, Messi's resilience has been tested through injuries, criticism, and the immense pressure of national expectations. Yet, his story teaches us the importance of perseverance, demonstrating how setbacks can be transformed into stepping stones towards success.

Messi's story is more than just a tale of athletic prowess; it's a guide on how to chase dreams with resilience, passion, and an unwavering belief in oneself, encouraging us all to pursue our goals with the idea that anything is possible

MOHAMED SALAH – BREAKING BARRIERS

"No one starts at the top. You have to climb the ladder just like everyone else."

- Mohamed Salah

CULTURAL BRIDGE

Mohamed Salah, often called "The Egyptian King," is a name that resonates across football stadiums with roaring applause and standing ovations. Hailing from Egypt, a country with rich traditions and deep history, Salah's journey to football stardom has inspired him to use his fame for good. He proudly shares his Muslim heritage with the world, breaking down barriers and fostering a spirit of tolerance among fans globally. His heartfelt celebrations and genuine interactions are lessons in respect and kindness, touching football supporters worldwide.

Mo Salah began his life in the small village of Nagrig in the Nile Delta. Born into a humble family, Salah's early life was not marked by luxury but by dreams of football glory. His father, a salesman, struggled financially, making higher education a distant dream for young Salah. Yet, it was the beautiful game of football where Salah saw his future.

From the age of 14, Salah's daily routine was gruelling. Every day, he embarked on a three-hour journey to Cairo, taking three different minibuses along bumpy dirt tracks to reach El Mokawloon football club. This six-hour round trip was a test of his resolve, but Salah's dream to become a football star kept his spirits high and his feet moving. His coaches had to place him on a special diet and training programme to help build his strength, and though the physical demands sometimes brought him to tears, these moments only fuelled his determination to improve and succeed.

Salah's breakthrough came when he shone on the international stage at the 2012 Olympics, catching the eye of scouts from across Europe. Soon after, he made a life-changing move to FC Basel in Switzerland - a daunting transition for the young Egyptian who had never before lived away from home. In Switzerland, Salah faced a whole new set of challenges. Language barriers and cultural differences made his early days particularly tough. Alone and unable to speak English or Swiss German, Salah spent many hours wandering the streets of Basel, trying to find his way in a completely foreign land.

Salah's second season at Basel saw him helping the team qualify for the Champions League, fulfilling one of his biggest dreams. His performances in Europe caught the eye of Chelsea, where he moved next, continuing his journey through different countries and leagues, including Italy, before finally landing at Liverpool.

REDS' BELOVED PHARAOH

When Mohamed Salah joined Liverpool in June 2017, grabbing the No. 11 jersey, he sparked an electric wave of excitement among fans. Salah's arrival at Liverpool was not just a transfer; it felt like a homecoming. The memories of playing as Liverpool legends in video games during his teenage years had always stayed with him, and now he was wearing the same red jersey, playing in front of the same passionate fans at

Anfield. The atmosphere he had adored from afar was now his reality.

Adapting to Liverpool's dynamic style of play was initially a challenge. The pace and rhythm were different from what he was used to in Rome, but Salah's determination and adaptability saw him swiftly find his feet. He quickly proved to be a footballing sensation, breaking records right from his debut season. With an impressive tally of 32 league goals, he not only captivated fans but also clinched the Premier League Golden Boot, outscoring legends like Barcelona's Lionel Messi and Tottenham's Harry Kane.

Salah's remarkable skills on the pitch earned him the prestigious PFA Players' Player of the Year award in April 2018. However, his first season had a bittersweet ending; during the Champions League final against Real Madrid, Salah suffered a left shoulder injury in a clash with Sergio Ramos. This was a devastating moment for Salah and Liverpool fans, as it significantly impacted the team's performance, leading to a loss in the final.

Undeterred by the previous year's setback, Salah returned stronger. In 2019, he played a crucial role in the Champions League final against Tottenham. Salah's early penalty goal set Liverpool on the path to a 2-0 victory, securing their first European trophy since 2005. The streets of Liverpool erupted in joy as Salah and his teammates paraded the Champions League trophy through the city.

The successes continued as Liverpool clinched their first Premier League title since 1990 in 2020, marking a historic moment for the club. Salah's contributions were pivotal in ending the 30-year wait for the league title. In 2022, Salah's consistent excellence was again recognised as he received his third Golden Boot award for being the league's top scorer. Additionally, his creative prowess was highlighted as he also won the Playmaker of the Season award after setting up 13 goals.

Salah's time at Liverpool has been a blend of personal triumphs and collective successes, making him not just a star player but a beloved figure at Anfield. Despite the challenge of understanding the local Scouse accent, which he finds particularly tricky, Salah feels deeply connected to the Liverpool supporters. Their songs and cheers uplift him during matches, filling him with pride and joy. Some standout chants include "Mohamed Salah, a gift from Allah" and "If he scores another few, then I'll be Muslim too," which are seen by some as a step against endemic racism in English football.

FAITH ON FIELD

Mohamed Salah has not only captivated fans with his spectacular football skills but has also emerged as a profound symbol of faith and cultural integration. Every goal he scores is marked by a serene moment of sujood — prostration — where he bows down in full view of tens of thousands. This act not only highlights his personal devotion but also broadcasts a powerful message about the importance of openly and proudly embracing one's culture and beliefs. Each time Salah performs sujood on the lush green of Anfield, the normally vibrant stadium quiets down, showing respect for his moment of reflection and the admiration he has garnered.

During Ramadan, the holy month of fasting for Muslims, Salah continues to deliver top performances despite not being able to eat or drink from dawn until sunset. This practice could easily affect a player's energy and health; however, Salah's commitment receives immense support from the entire Liverpool organisation. His teammates make sure he gets the necessary nutrition after sunset to maintain his performance without compromising his spiritual observance.

Salah's open expression of faith has profoundly impacted not only the football community but also wider British society. His popularity has helped challenge and reshape stereotypes about

Muslims. Mo Salah, a North African and a Muslim, is not just accepted in Britain but adored, presenting a positive image of Muslims. He demonstrates that a Muslim can be both a celebrated sports icon and a proud practitioner of his faith. By living his faith openly, Salah has bridged cultural gaps and shown that sports can be a powerful medium for promoting respect across diverse communities.

PRIDE OF THE NILE

Mohamed Salah, often hailed as the "Fourth Pyramid" or the "Pride of the Arabs," is not just a footballer but a national hero in Egypt. His spectacular performances on the pitch and his profound impact off it have elevated him to a status akin to a cultural landmark, deeply embedded in the heart of every Egyptian.

Salah's crowning moment for Egypt came during the World Cup qualifiers, where his coolly taken, last-minute penalty against Congo not only won the match but also secured Egypt's place in the World Cup for the first time since

1990. The scenes in Alexandria were jubilant as Salah, with a grin that stretched across his face, was joyously hoisted onto the shoulders of fans and paraded around the stadium. This moment of triumph sparked celebrations across the nation, cementing his status as a national treasure in the hearts of the Egyptian people.

In Cairo, Salah's presence is ubiquitous. His face graces numerous murals and walls across the city, with one such mural outside a downtown cafe becoming a beloved tourist attraction. Markets teem with merchandise bearing his likeness, from bed linen to lanterns, showing just how deeply ingrained he is in the cultural fabric of Egypt.

But Salah's impact extends beyond his footballing achievements. His commitment to philanthropy has endeared him even more to his compatriots. From donating machines to local hospitals to funding the construction of a sewage treatment plant in his hometown of Nagrig, Salah's generosity has improved countless lives. He has also invested in public infrastructure, renovating sports centres, schools, and mosques, and even setting up an ambulance service, showcasing his dedication to giving back to the community that raised him.

Salah's influence was humorously highlighted during the country's presidential election, where despite not being a candidate, one million Egyptians showed their adoration by spoiling their ballots to write his name, a testament to the immense respect and love he commands nationwide.

Beyond his charitable efforts, Salah has used his platform to champion social causes, notably advocating for the improvement of women's rights in the Middle East. He has been vocal about the need for cultural change, emphasising that men in the Muslim world should treat women with greater respect and equality. His public statements on these issues have sparked conversations and have shown him to be a progressive figure not just in sports but also in social issues.

CELEBRATING UNITY

Mo Salah's story is a powerful example of how sports can bridge cultural divides and inspire positive change. His journey shows us that staying true to oneself and respecting others can transform a talented athlete into a cherished hero, both at home and abroad.

Growing up in a small village in Egypt, he played football not just for fun, but with a burning desire to do something great. That dream didn't make him forget where he came from; instead, it fuelled his passion to represent his country and culture with pride on the global stage.

Salah's famous goal celebrations, where he kneels in gratitude, teach us about humility and the importance of staying grounded, no matter how high you rise. This act, seen by millions around the world, does more than just celebrate a goal; it shares a piece of his culture, teaching us that our differences can be sources of pride and celebration.

Salah's story encourages us to stand proud of who we are, embracing our roots while reaching for the stars. Being a hero isn't just about what you achieve on your own, but about lifting others up and paving the way for future generations. With a ball at your feet and determination in your heart, you can not only change the game but also the world around you.

CRISTIANO RONALDO – UNYIELDING DETERMINATION

"Dreams are not what you see in your sleep, dreams are things which do not let you sleep."

- Cristiano Ronaldo

DREAMS BEGIN IN MADEIRA

Cristiano Ronaldo's story begins on the small, picturesque island of Madeira, Portugal. Imagine a place so beautiful, with the bluest oceans and greenest hills you've ever seen – that's where Cristiano grew up. Even as a little boy, Cristiano had big dreams. He loved football more than anything else. Every day after school, he'd race to the nearest field, his feet barely touching the ground. He played with an old, patched-up ball, but in his eyes, it was the most precious treasure. Football wasn't just a game for Cristiano; it was his world. The passion in his heart was as vast as the ocean surrounding Madeira.

Cristiano's family didn't have a lot of money; living in a tiny home, he shared a room with his siblings. His mum and dad worked incredibly hard to take care of the children, but sometimes life threw curveballs their way. His dad struggled with health issues, which was tough for the whole family. But instead of letting these challenges slow him down, Cristiano used them as fuel to ignite an even greater desire to succeed. He knew that to make his family proud he had to give his all to football, the game he loved more than anything.

When Cristiano was just eight years old, his talent on the football field began to shine like a lighthouse guiding ships home. He started playing for a local team, Andorinha, where his father worked as a kit man. But Cristiano's skill was too big for just one team; soon, he moved to Nacional, one of the top teams in Madeira. He wasn't just playing; he was sprinting like a cheetah, and striking the ball with the power of a cannon. His dreams were getting bigger with each goal he scored, each game he played. People started to notice this young boy who played football with the joy and passion of someone who loved every minute on the field.

Cristiano's dedication to football was unmatched. He was always practising under the sun until it dipped below the horizon. Even when others were resting, Cristiano was working, perfecting his dribbles, his shots, and his speed. This wasn't just hard work - it was his heart's work. Every drop of sweat on the training field was a step closer to making his family's life better.

THE JOURNEY THROUGH HARDSHIP

Cristiano's resolve, shaped by the personal challenges he faced, pushed him to aim higher, run faster, and strike stronger. By the time he was just 12 years old, something amazing happened. Sporting Lisbon, one of the biggest football clubs in Portugal, invited him to join their academy. This was a dream come true, but it also meant leaving his family and his beloved island home. Imagine having to say goodbye to everything you know at such a young age, all because you're chasing a dream. But Cristiano was brave. He packed his bags, hugged his family, and set off to Lisbon. It was hard, but inside his heart, he knew this was his chance to do something great.

Joining Sporting Lisbon's academy wasn't just a step towards becoming a professional football player; it was a leap into his future, a future filled with goals, victories, and the chance to become one of the greatest football players the world has ever seen.

THE MAKING OF A LEGEND

At Sporting Lisbon, Ronaldo dazzled everyone with his fast feet and unbelievable skills, scoring goals that made people sit up and take notice. Then came a moment that would change Cristiano's life forever. In a friendly match against Manchester United, Cristiano's performance was so impressive that it left everyone, including the opposing players, in awe. Sir Alex Ferguson, the legendary manager of Manchester United, knew right then that Cristiano had to be his player. In 2003, Cristiano made the move to Manchester United, stepping onto a bigger stage and into a new chapter of his life.

Under Sir Alex Ferguson's guidance, Cristiano found not just a coach, but a mentor and a father figure who believed in him and pushed him to achieve his full potential. Ronaldo blossomed into a footballer of extraordinary calibre, with his dazzling dribbles, powerful shots, and an aerial ability that defied physics. At United, Ronaldo's talent was undeniable, highlighted by his stunning 40-yard goal against Porto in the Champions League, a moment that showcased his ability to seize the spotlight on the grandest stages.

During his time at Manchester United, Cristiano's trophy case quickly filled with prestigious awards, including three Premier League titles and a Champions League trophy in 2008. It was here that Ronaldo honed his iconic free-kick technique, becoming feared and revered for his ability to curve the ball with precision and power. His work ethic set him apart, often the first to arrive at training and the last to leave, driven by an insatiable desire to improve and conquer.

The next chapter of Ronaldo's illustrious career unfolded at Real Madrid, where he elevated his game to new heights. At Madrid, Ronaldo's name became synonymous with success, leading the club to an impressive four Champions League titles, including an unprecedented three consecutive wins. His time at Real Madrid not only cemented his status as one of the game's all-time greats but also showcased his evolution into a more complete player, combining his trademark speed and skill with a remarkable goal-scoring instinct.

TURNING CHALLENGES INTO TRIUMPHS

Cristiano Ronaldo, a name that echoes in the halls of football greatness, hasn't always had an easy path. Imagine being told you're too focused on looking good, too "glamorous" to be a serious athlete. But guess what? Cristiano didn't let those words slow him down. Instead, he used them as fuel to show the world that being dedicated to your appearance and being an incredible football player aren't mutually exclusive. He proved that taking pride in all aspects of your life, including looking your best, can go hand in hand with winning matches. Cristiano's response to criticism was to work even harder, to believe in himself even more, and to dedicate himself to being the best football player he could be.

One of the most exciting parts of Cristiano's career has been his intense rivalry with Lionel Messi. This rivalry is like a superhero battle in the world of sports, pushing both players to new heights. This rivalry wasn't about bitterness; it was about mutual respect and the drive to excel. Every goal Messi scored, Ronaldo was inspired to score two. It's a perfect example of how having someone to challenge you can make you reach even higher, turning rivalry into a stepping stone for personal growth.

Cristiano's journey didn't stop in Europe; his latest adventure has taken him to Saudi Arabia, where he's continued to shine. This move surprised many, but Ronaldo has continued to show his incredible skill and dedication to the sport. Playing for Al Nassr, Cristiano has shown that his passion for football knows no bounds, embracing a new culture with open arms. At the age of 39, he's scored breathtaking goals and inspired other players with his relentless work ethic, self-belief, and commitment to excellence.

DETERMINATION DRIVES SUCCESS

Cristiano Ronaldo's journey to football stardom is a tale of unyielding determination and incredible hard work. From his early days in Madeira, Portugal, Cristiano faced challenges that could have stopped many in their tracks, but instead of letting them defeat him, he used them as fuel to push himself even harder. Ronaldo's story teaches us that with hard work, self-belief, and dedication, you can overcome criticism, turn rivalry into motivation, and achieve greatness, no matter where you are in the world.

Let Cristiano's journey encourage you to dream big, work hard, and never let anything stand in the way of reaching your goals. Remember, your determination and discipline are the keys to unlocking your potential and achieving your own version of success. Someday, you might just inspire someone else with your own incredible story.

SON HEUNG-MIN –
SERVING THE NATION

*"I want to make my country proud every time
I step onto the pitch."*

- Son Heung-min

FROM DRILLS TO GLOBAL THRILLS

In the electrifying world of football, where legends are born and heroes are made, there shines a star from South Korea, Son Heung-min. Known for his dazzling speed, brilliant footwork, and an unbreakable spirit, Son is celebrated not just as a phenomenal player but as a dedicated son of his nation, whose love for the game is as deep as his love for his homeland.

Son's early years were shaped by his father, Son Woong-jung, a retired footballer turned visionary coach, whose rigorous training and strict coaching forged Son into the player he is today. Under his father's watchful eye, Son's journey was anything but ordinary. His father was a strict coach, demanding perfection and discipline, qualities that shaped Son into the relentless force he is today. Imagine juggling a football for three whole laps without letting it touch the ground. This was just one of the many challenging drills Son had to master. Despite the tough love, Son's respect and admiration for his father are boundless, knowing that every drop of sweat was a step closer to his dreams.

In South Korea, where education often overshadows athletics, Son dared to dream differently. As a ball boy in FC Seoul matches, Son idolised Korean players in the Premier League, dreaming of one day joining their ranks. His move to Germany to join Hamburger SV at the tender age of 16 marked the beginning of an extraordinary adventure. Through sheer determination and a unique method of learning German by watching animated films, Son adapted to a new country and its football culture.

Being one of the few Asian faces in European leagues, Son has battled not just opponents on the field but also prejudice off it. Faced with the stereotype that Asian players couldn't match up to their European counterparts, Son has not just challenged this view; he's demolished it, game after game. His success is a loud, clear message to clubs around the world: talent knows no race, and determination speaks in every language.

SPRINTING TOWARDS GREATNESS

In the summer of 2015, a new chapter began for Son. With a dream move, Son joined Tottenham for a groundbreaking £22 million, shattering records as the most expensive Asian player in history. Imagine the excitement, the anticipation as Tottenham's Chairman Daniel Levy, determined, flew to Leverkusen in his private helicopter, ensuring that Son would wear the iconic white jersey of Spurs.

In his debut season, Son's name echoed in the stands as he netted 12 goals, but that was just the beginning. The following season, he took his game to astronomical heights, scoring 21 goals across all competitions and propelling Tottenham to their highest finish in 54 years. It was clear: Son was not just a player; he was a phenomenon, rewriting history and setting new standards with every match. Eventually, the 2021 season saw Son etch his name in the annals of history as he clinched the Premier League Golden Boot alongside Mo Salah with 23 goals, becoming the first Asian player to achieve this monumental feat. It was a testament to his relentless work ethic, his unyielding spirit, and his insatiable appetite for goals.

Son's brilliance on the field earned him also a special place in Premier League history as the first Asian to win the Player of the Month award, not once but twice in a single season. But his ambitions were loftier still. With determination in his heart and magic in his boots, Son played a pivotal role in Tottenham's journey to their first-ever Champions League final, showcasing his talent on Europe's grandest stage and proving that he was among the world's elite.

The partnership between Son and Harry Kane became the stuff of legend, a dynamic duo that struck fear into the hearts of defenders. Their incredible synergy on the pitch led them to match a Premier League record, combining for

13 goals in just 17 league games during the 2020-2021 season. It was a partnership built on mutual respect and a shared drive for excellence.

In a fitting tribute to his dedication, and incredible impact on and off the pitch, Son was named Tottenham's new captain in August 2023, succeeding Hugo Lloris. With the captain's armband came new responsibilities, but Son rose to the challenge with grace and determination. In a stunning display of leadership and skill, he scored his first hat-trick as club captain in a 5-2 triumph over Burnley, demonstrating that his commitment to the team was as unwavering as ever.

FOOTBALL AND SERVICE

In South Korea, every male citizen faces a call to duty, a requirement to serve in the military for 18 months. This is a tradition that speaks volumes about dedication and patriotism, a duty that binds the hearts of the nation's youth. But imagine being at the peak of your football career, scoring goals, living your dream, and facing the possibility of stepping away from the field to fulfil this duty. This was the reality for Son Heung-min, South Korea's football sensation.

But in 2018, an opportunity emerged that would allow Son to fulfil his duty and continue his journey in football: the Asian Games held in Indonesia. The stakes were high, as victory in the games meant more than just a medal; it offered an exemption from the traditional military service, allowing athletes like Son to dedicate their prime years to their sport. With determination in his heart and his eyes on the prize, Son played with unparalleled passion, leading his team to glory as they clinched the gold medal. This victory was a triumph on the field and a turning point in Son's life, granting him the exemption he needed to continue enchanting fans at Tottenham Hotspur.

But Son's story of duty didn't end with the exemption. When the world paused in the face of the COVID-19 pandemic, and football fields lay silent, Son saw an opportunity not to rest, but to serve. Even though he could have skipped military service, Son chose to stand shoulder to shoulder with his compatriots, undergoing basic military training. For weeks, Son traded his football kit for a military uniform, undergoing the same rigorous training that shapes soldiers, showing that beneath the superstar athlete beats the heart of a dedicated citizen.

THE WINNING GOAL OF GIVING BACK

Son's story resonates with the values of duty and service that are celebrated in British heroes throughout history. Just like soldiers, firefighters, doctors, and teachers dedicate their lives to serving the country and its people, Son Heung-min showed that athletes too can play a significant role in contributing to their nation's pride and well-being.

Son's journey teaches us that being a hero isn't just about scoring the winning goal or being the best on the field. It's about answering the call of duty with courage, making sacrifices for the good of others, and always putting the team, community, or country ahead of oneself. Remember that greatness comes not just from talent but from the heart, the courage to serve, and the willingness to put the greater good above all else.

DIDIER DROGBA –
A GOAL FOR PEACE

"I have won many trophies in my time, but nothing will ever top helping win the battle for peace in my country."

- Didier Drogba

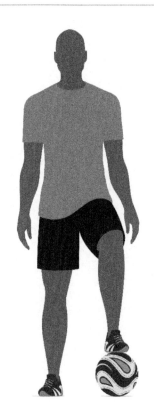

Didier Drogba's story begins in the vibrant heart of Côte d'Ivoire, where the love for football runs as deep as the rivers that cross the land. Growing up, Didier's world was filled with the sounds of cheering crowds from local football matches, and the dusty fields of his neighbourhood were the first stages of his dreams. These fields weren't just patches of earth; they were where Didier first imagined scoring goals in stadiums filled with thousands of fans. Life in Côte d'Ivoire, with its rich culture and tight-knit communities also presented challenges, such as limited resources and access to professional training, which made the dream of becoming a football star seem like a distant reality.

The next chapter of Didier's journey unfolded when his family moved to France, a transition that brought about its own set of challenges. It was tough; the cold weather, the unfamiliar food, and the feeling of being an outsider in a new country. Yet, Didier's family instilled in him the values of resilience and the importance of sticking together through hard times.

Starting his career in France, Didier quickly made an impact, not just as a player who could score goals, but as someone who played passionate and fierce. He played for several French teams, each time lacing up his boots with the dream of one day playing on the world's biggest football stages. It was during these formative years that Didier learned to blend the raw talent he brought from Côte d'Ivoire with the discipline and technique that European football demanded. His time in France was like a training ground, preparing him for the biggest leap of his career – joining Chelsea, one of England's most prestigious football clubs.

SCORING DREAMS IN BLUE

Drogba's journey with Chelsea was marked by incredible achievements, including winning several Premier League titles and multiple FA Cups, where his goals often led the team to glory. But among all these moments, it was his pivotal role in Chelsea's 2012 Champions League triumph that truly cemented his legacy in the hearts of football fans everywhere.

The 2012 Champions League final was like the final scene of a dramatic sports film, with Chelsea facing off against Bayern Munich in a match that had fans on the edge of their seats. Didier was the star of the show, first scoring a powerful header that tied the match and sent it into extra time, then stepping up to take the decisive penalty kick in the shootout. Imagine the pressure, the entire stadium holding its breath as Didier placed the ball on the spot. With a confident run, he struck the ball perfectly into the net, securing Chelsea's first ever Champions League title. It was a moment of pure magic, the kind of story you'd read in a book and dream about, but for Didier and Chelsea fans, it was wonderfully real.

During his amazing time at Chelsea, Didier Drogba did more than just help his team win lots of trophies. He played football in a way that made people's jaws drop, combining power, precision, and an undeniable flair. His ability to score from almost anywhere on the pitch, whether with a free kick, a powerful header or a delicate flick, made him one of the most feared strikers in the world. Imagine a player who could hold off the toughest defenders with his sheer strength, then dance past them with the elegance of a ballet dancer, and you've got Didier Drogba. But it wasn't just his physical attributes that set him apart; it was his leadership and his heart, always playing with a fire that inspired both teammates and fans.

THE STRIKER WHO UNITED A COUNTRY

Didier Drogba became more than just a football player for Côte d'Ivoire; he became a national hero. In the heart of Africa, where the sun kisses the earth and the air vibrates with the cheers of football fans, his incredible skill led Côte d'Ivoire to the global stage of football. When Drogba and his team qualified for their first

World Cup in 2006, it was like a dream come true for the entire country. Imagine the streets of Côte d'Ivoire, buzzing with excitement, as people of all ages celebrated this historic moment.

But Drogba's influence stretched far beyond the football pitch. During a time when Côte d'Ivoire was torn apart by civil war, Drogba did something extraordinary. With the eyes of the world upon him, he made a heartfelt plea to the combatants, asking them to lay down their arms for the sake of peace. And guess what? They listened to him! His words, filled with genuine concern and love for his homeland, touched the hearts of many, leading to a ceasefire. In a land where football is not just a game but a lifeline, a way to forget the struggles of daily life, Drogba's plea was a powerful reminder of what truly matters - peace, unity, and the well-being of one's country. He united Côte d'Ivoire in a way few could, transforming the spirit of the nation.

His unwavering commitment to peace has made him a legend not just in Africa, but around the world. But Didier didn't stop there. He donated the entire $5 million signing bonus from his endorsement deal with Pepsi towards the construction of a new hospital in Abidjan, the largest city in Côte d'Ivoire. It opened up a world of better health care for thousands of people, providing them with access to medical services they might not have had before.

Drogba has also been a relentless fighter against malaria, a disease that affects millions of people in Africa. He himself suffered from malaria but turned his personal battle into a public campaign to raise awareness and fight the disease. By teaming up with health organisations, Didier used his fame to educate people about prevention methods, treatment options, and the importance of clean environments to reduce the spread of malaria. His campaigns have helped save lives and have brought much-needed attention to health issues that often go unnoticed by the wider world.

THE POWER OF SPORTS TO CHANGE LIVES

Sports aren't just about winning matches or scoring the most points; they have a special magic that can bring people together, no matter where they come from or what they believe in. Drogba has inspired people in Africa and all over the world to look at football in a new way. Through his actions, he has shown us that sports have the power to heal communities and inspire peace.

So, the next time you play your favourite sport or engage in your favourite activity, remember Didier Drogba's story. You have the power to make a difference. Whether it's standing up for a friend, helping out in your community, or just spreading kindness, every action counts. It all begins with a single step — or in Drogba's case, a single goal.

FRANCESCO TOTTI – LOYALTY PERSONIFIED

"I never played for money or fame. I played for the love of the game and the pride of representing AS Roma."

- Francesco Totti

In the heart of Italy's ancient city, Rome, where stories of gladiators and emperors whisper through the ruins, there lived a footballer whose story is as legendary as the Colosseum itself. Francesco Totti, known as the heart and soul of AS Roma, is a name that echoes through the cobblestone streets, not just for his incredible talent but also for his extraordinary loyalty to his beloved club. Imagine dedicating your entire career to the team you've loved since you were a child, becoming a symbol of pride for the entire city. That's what Totti did for AS Roma, embodying the spirit of dedication and passion.

From the time he was just a little boy, Totti had one dream – to play for AS Roma. Every night, he'd go to bed dreaming of wearing the iconic maroon and gold jersey, representing his city and the club that captured his heart. From the moment he joined the youth team of AS Roma, his extraordinary talent was clear. It wasn't long before he was called up to join the first team, a moment as exciting as unwrapping the best present you could imagine. And then came the day he was handed the number 10 jersey — a symbol of trust, responsibility, and greatness. Wearing number 10 wasn't just about being a player; it was about becoming a leader, a creator, and the heart of the team.

TIMELESS NUMBER 10

For an astonishing 25 years, Totti dedicated his heart, his soul, and his unparalleled talent to the team of the Eternal City. Starting in 1999, Totti took on the role of captain, a position he held with pride and honour. Throughout his career, his roles on the pitch evolved — from a playmaker with a vision that could cut through defences, to a striker whose goals were poetry in motion, and finally, as a super sub, a role that showcased his enduring class and influence on the game, even in the twilight of his career.

Among his crowning achievements, Totti led AS Roma to the Serie A title in the 2000-2001 season, a triumph that had fans dancing in the streets of Rome. It was a season of dreams, with Totti at the heart of it all, scoring goals, creating opportunities, and inspiring his team to reach for the stars.

Francesco Totti, The Golden Boy, The Eighth King of Rome, The Gladiator... Like a masterful centurion leading his troops, Totti was a player whose skills were a blend of hard work, unselfish play, and a dazzling array of manoeuvres that could outwit any defence. Under the guidance of coach Zeman, Totti underwent a transformation worthy of the myths of old. He embraced the rigorous demands of 21st-century football, engaging in a muscle-strengthening programme that fortified him for the challenges of the modern game. This evolution added strength, stamina, and an explosive shooting power to his arsenal, even as it traded a bit of his speed and agility.

In a world where players often chase after bigger contracts or more prestigious clubs, Totti's heart remained rooted in Rome. Offers came and went, but Totti stayed, his bond with AS Roma unbreakable. He became more than just a player; he was the club's undying spirit. The number 10 jersey, a symbol of football royalty, was Totti's mantle, a fitting tribute to his genius on the field. In 2017, AS Roma retired his jersey number 10 as an eternal homage to his contributions, ensuring that no other player would wear it again.

CELEBRATIONS, CHARITY, AND CHILDREN

Francesco Totti stands out not just for his incredible skills on the field but also for his vibrant personality off it. This Roman legend also had a knack for bringing smiles to fans' faces, whether through his playful goal celebrations or his heartfelt charitable work.

Imagine the stadium buzzing with anticipation, the score tight, and then Totti scores! But it's not just the goal that gets fans roaring; it's what comes next. Totti was famous for his exuberant celebrations, often revealing T-shirts with humorous messages. One memorable moment was in 2012 when, after ending a scoring drought against Chievo, he flashed a T-shirt that read *"Scusate il Ritardo"* ("Sorry for the delay"). It was his way of apologising to fans for waiting so long to see him score again. But perhaps the most viral of his celebrations was when he scored twice against Lazio in the Derby della Capitale. Not content with just a goal, Totti took a selfie with the Roma fans in the background, capturing a moment of joy and unity that would spread across the globe.

Beyond the stadium lights and roaring crowds, Totti showed his golden heart through his work with children. In 2003, he became a goodwill ambassador for UNICEF, using his fame to shine a light on the needs of children around the world. Two years later, he became an ambassador for the FIFA/SOS Children's Villages, dedicating himself to making a difference in the lives of abandoned children. Totti even published two best-selling joke books, with all proceeds going to charity. These weren't just any jokes; they were self-effacing ones that locals told about him and his teammates.

In 2009, Totti took his charitable efforts to the next level by launching a campaign to promote Football Adopting Abandoned Children. He adopted a team of eleven young Kenyans, aiming to play football in Nairobi and coach them along their journey. It was a project close to Totti's heart, combining his love for football with his commitment to helping children in need.

DREAMING BIG AND STAYING TRUE

In the grand adventure of football, where every pass, goal, and game tells a story, there shines a tale of Francesco Totti, a true hero of the sport. His journey with AS Roma, a story of unwavering loyalty and dedication, teaches us all an important lesson: sticking with what you love, through thick and thin, can lead to incredible success.

So, as you lace up your boots, remember Francesco Totti's lesson. Be dedicated, be loyal, and above all, believe in yourself. Just like Totti did on the football pitch, you too can achieve greatness by staying true to your heart and never giving up on what you love.

MARCUS RASHFORD – COMMUNITY CHAMPION

" When you come from a place of struggle, it inspires you to make a change for others."

- Marcus Rashford

In the shadow of Manchester's gleaming skyline lies a story of grit, determination, and the incredible journey of a young football prodigy named Marcus Rashford. Rising from the challenging streets, Marcus's tale is one of triumph over adversity, a vivid reminder of the power of dreams and the impact an individual can wield, not just in sport but in the very fabric of society.

Marcus's beginnings were humble, to say the least. Born into a working-class family, life was a daily struggle. Melanie, his mother, juggled three jobs to keep the home fires burning. A cashier by day at a betting shop and a cleaner by night, she did everything within her power to provide for Marcus and his siblings. Yet, despite her efforts, there were nights when the cupboard was bare, nights when her children ate and she did not.

The support systems that Marcus and his family relied on were vital. Breakfast clubs, free school meals, and visits to food banks were not just helping hands; they were lifelines. Marcus's day would begin with the school's breakfast club, a vital source of nourishment that would power him through the day until he could return home to his mother's embrace.

For young Marcus, the echo of an empty stomach was a call to action, a drive that propelled him forward. From these trials, a relentless spirit was forged. He saw in his struggles not a barrier but a motivator, pushing him to excel on the football pitch. On the football field, Marcus was a revelation. With every dash down the pitch, every electrifying goal, and every match-winning performance, he carried with him the hopes and dreams of his family, his community, and countless young boys and girls facing their own battles.

Drawing from his own experiences, Marcus became a relentless advocate for the underprivileged, wielding his platform with grace and determination. His campaign against child food poverty was a rallying cry that united a nation, showcasing the profound impact an athlete can have on society.

GRASSROOTS TO GREATNESS

Marcus's journey started at Fletcher Moss Rangers, a community club where a five-year-old Rashford, albeit scrawny, displayed a passion and energy for football that was simply unmatched. His talent was undeniable, and by the age of seven, Manchester United, along with other top clubs, had spotted his potential. By eleven, Marcus was making history, becoming the youngest player ever selected for Manchester United's Schoolboy Scholars scheme, a clear sign that this young talent was on a fast track to greatness.

Marcus's football wasn't confined to structured academy play. He thrived in the raw, competitive world of five-a-side tournaments across Manchester, where the stakes were high, and the play was fierce. Winning these tournaments meant more than just claiming victory; it allowed Marcus to earn enough prize money to buy a ticket to watch Manchester United play at Old Trafford. For Marcus, Old Trafford was more than a stadium – it was a dream, a place that felt like home. His triumphs in these tournaments were steps towards belonging, towards realising his dream of playing in those hallowed grounds as a Manchester United player.

Despite tempting offers from other clubs that promised a life of luxury and ease for his family, Rashford's heart and dreams were tethered to United. He knew that true success wasn't about financial gain but about achieving one's dreams and changing lives through the sport he loved. His determination was unwavering, fuelled by the belief that he belonged among the best, not just in the academy but on the first team alongside legends like Rooney and Ronaldo.

His commitment and passion paid off when, at just 16, he trained with United's first team for the first time. And then came the unforgettable night of 25 February 2016. Due to an injury crisis at United, Rashford was called up to the first team for a Europa League match against Midtjylland. What followed was nothing short of a fairy tale: Rashford scored twice on his debut, announcing himself to the world with a performance that was both breathtaking and inspirational. Just days later, Rashford made his Premier League debut against Arsenal, again scoring twice and assisting another in a victory that would make headlines around the world.

As a fresh-faced youngster, Rashford earned his spot on the senior team under the guidance of new manager José Mourinho, who handed him the number 19 shirt in his 2016-17 breakthrough season. Rashford's prowess on the field was soon recognised as he finished runner-up for the Golden Boy award, marking him as one of Europe's finest young talents.

The following seasons saw Rashford don the prestigious number 10 shirt, signifying his growing importance at the club. He continued to deliver magical moments, like his double against Liverpool and his vital contributions in the Champions League. Despite the pressure and the arrival of high-profile teammates, Rashford's star only shone brighter.

Under the guidance of new boss Erik ten Hag, Rashford began to shine brighter. Positioned as a dynamic centre-forward and sometimes as a crafty left-winger, he scored crucial goals against tough teams like Liverpool and Arsenal, showing his versatility and sharp football brain. His hard work paid off when he scored his 100th goal for Manchester United, joining the ranks of legends.

Rashford's outstanding 2022-2023 season was capped by helping his team clinch the 2023 EFL Cup, where his goal sealed the victory. His phenomenal form earned him accolades from teammates and fans alike, bagging the Sir Matt Busby Player of the Year and the Players' Player of the Year awards.

FIGHT AGAINST POVERTY

Marcus Rashford is not just a star on the football pitch but also a champion off it, leading a formidable charge against child hunger in the UK. Recognising the hardship faced by many families similar to his own, Rashford was stunned to discover the vast number of children suffering from hunger nationwide. Moved by visits to his old primary school, where he saw the situation worsening, Rashford knew he had to take action.

During the COVID-19 lockdown in March 2020, when schools shut down, Rashford feared for the millions of children who relied on free school meals as their main source of nutrition. He teamed up with FareShare, a charity combating food waste and hunger, to ensure that children wouldn't go hungry. Starting with a substantial personal donation, his involvement quickly turned into a nationwide campaign. He helped the charity raise over £20 million, providing three million meals to children across the UK who were missing out on their school lunches.

But Rashford didn't stop there. He took his fight right to the top, penning an open letter to the UK government, pushing for an extension of free school meal provisions during the school summer holidays. This heartfelt appeal led to a government U-turn, securing meals for 1.3 million children during the school break, a move that was both a victory for Rashford and the families it aided.

Fuelled by his childhood experiences of food poverty, Rashford then set up the Child Food Poverty Task Force, collaborating with food giants, charities, and delivery companies to tackle child food poverty on a grand scale. The task force lobbied the government for sustained support, highlighting that nearly four million children were living in poverty and many were skipping meals. His advocacy challenged politicians and the public alike to confront uncomfortable truths about inequality and poverty in one of the world's richest countries.

As the voice of the campaign, Rashford wasn't just a figurehead; he was actively involved, inspiring others to join the fight. Despite facing criticism from some quarters, Rashford remained focused, driven by a simple yet powerful belief: no child should go to bed hungry. He leveraged his platform, combining his status as a footballer and his personal experiences, to champion the needs of underprivileged children, making hunger and poverty issues impossible to ignore.

SCORING GOALS FOR SOCIAL CHANGE

Marcus's actions teach us several important lessons. First, there's the power of empathy — understanding and sharing the feelings of others. Marcus didn't forget his roots or the struggles he faced; instead, he used his experiences to connect with and help others.

Next is the importance of taking action. Marcus saw a problem and didn't sit back; he stepped up to make a change. Whether it's helping a friend, volunteering, or speaking up about something you believe in, remember that like Marcus, you too can make a difference.

Lastly, Marcus teaches us about leadership. True leaders aren't just the ones who score goals or get the best marks; they're the ones who see a need, take action, and inspire others to join them in making a positive impact.

So, next time you're on the playground or working on a group project, think about how you can use your own strengths, just like Marcus Rashford, to help others and lead by example. Whether you're scoring goals, helping friends, or standing up for what's right, remember that even the smallest actions can make a big difference in the world. Marcus Rashford isn't just scoring goals; he's setting them for all of us to achieve greatness, both on and off the field.

IAN WRIGHT – UNLIKELY HERO

"Life is like football: you need goals; if there are no goals in your life then you can't win."

- Ian Wright

TOUGH CHALLENGES

In the tight-knit streets of South London, where the echoes of bouncing footballs rang against the backdrop of sprawling council estates, young Ian Wright was dreaming big. His dream? To become a professional footballer. Ian's playground was the concrete courtyards and patchy fields of his neighbourhood, where he mastered his kicks, despite the lack of lush green pitches or fancy gear.

The third son of Jamaican immigrants, Ian's early life was not one of luxury. After his father left when Ian was just four, his mother struggled to raise him and his siblings in a challenging environment. At home, life was tough. Ian's new stepdad was a harsh figure, the sort of man who would gamble away his wages, come home late, and create tension in the cramped one-bedroom home. Ian often felt singled out for the worst treatment, receiving hand-me-downs while his siblings got new clothes and enduring the brunt of his stepdad's cruelty.

Football became Ian's refuge from the daily struggles. In the shadow of massive brick walls peppered with 'NO BALL GAMES' signs and angry dads threatening to slice a football that dared bounce off their cars, Ian and his friends would kick about, making the most of every chance to play their beloved game. However, the aggression from his home life sometimes spilled onto the pitch. If provoked or embarrassed, Ian's frustration would erupt, leading to scraps and scuffles during games. His brother Maurice would even caution others, hinting at Ian's fierce temper if challenged too harshly.

In school too, Ian was a misunderstood child known among teachers for his restless energy and was frequently sent outside, left to watch his classmates through the glass as they continued their lessons without him.

It was in one of these quiet, reflective moments outside the classroom that Mr. Pigden, a strict yet perceptive teacher, noticed something in Ian that others hadn't seen. A former war pilot with a commanding presence, Mr. Pigden saw beyond the disruptive behaviour to a boy who was lost in the school system but had potential waiting to be unlocked. One pivotal day, Mr. Pigden stopped and invited Ian to come with him, changing the course of his life forever.

Under Mr. Pigden's wing, Ian found a sanctuary in the school library, a place where he was not just another troublesome student but a young boy with responsibilities and talents. Mr. Pigden taught him not just academics but life skills — patience, confidence, and the art of communication. He explained why Ian often felt so angry and how to channel those feelings positively. Recognising Ian's passion for football, Mr. Pigden discussed tactics and even played a role in refining Ian's approach to the game, advising him to focus on finesse rather than force.

You know that warm feeling you get inside when you've made somebody proud? You can't buy that. Ian grew up wanting to get that from his dad or his stepdad and never got it.

TURNING POINT

Ian's football journey kicked off at age 11 when he first trotted off to trials with a fiery gleam of hope in his eyes. But reality proved harsh, as door after door closed on him. Every club he tried out for sent him away – unchosen and unnoticed. Eleven long years of relentless rejections can weigh heavily on a person's spirit, shaping them in profound ways. But each 'no' from the likes of Arsenal, Chelsea, and many other clubs wasn't just a missed opportunity – it was a harsh reminder of the mountain he still had to climb.

One particularly grim day found him sitting alone in a club reception area in Brighton, clinging to the last shreds of hope he had left. He was utterly broke, not even having the cash for a train ticket back to London.

Life took twists and turns, and a minor run-in with the law over unpaid parking fines saw Ian spending a few weeks behind bars. It was a stark wake-up call, pushing him to rethink his path. As he approached his 22nd birthday, Ian decided it was time to 'settle down'. Undeterred but realistic, he chose to lay bricks and plaster walls, a far cry from scoring goals. While contemporaries like Messi and Mbappé were already collecting trophies on global stages at the age of 22, and Gerrard and Ødegaard were captaining their teams, Ian Wright was nowhere near the professional pitches.

Yet, the dream of football glory never truly faded, simmering within him. Crystal Palace, a club he hadn't dared hope would notice him, offered him a trial. Incredulous but with nothing to lose, Ian seized this opportunity with both hands. He played with everything he had, as if making up for lost time. After a nerve-wracking performance where every pass and shot felt like his last, the unimaginable happened. The coach, moved by Ian's determination and skill, pulled him aside after the match and offered him a three-month professional contract.

This wasn't just any contract – it was a transformation that felt both exhilarating and redemptive. As he signed the papers, the reality of his new life began to sink in. Ian Wright, the boy who had faced a barrage of rejections, who had known the inside of a prison cell, who had felt the sting of bullying and the weight of defeat, was finally a professional footballer. When Ian called his mum from the club's office to tell her the news, her tears through the phone line spoke volumes. They were tears of relief, of pride, and of joy — a mother's love pouring out for her son who had, against all odds, turned his wildest dreams into reality.

HEART OF A LION

At Crystal Palace, Ian's formidable partnership with Mark Bright was instrumental in lifting the team to new heights. Together, they formed a striking duo that terrorised defences across the country. At Palace, Ian was more than a goal-scorer; he was a motivator who could turn the game on its head. His energy was infectious, his passion unmistakable. In the 1989 season, Ian led a dazzling charge to the FA Cup final, a feat that etched his name into the hearts of fans.

In 1991, when Ian joined Arsenal, he brought with him not just his skills but a spirit that breathed new life into the team. At Arsenal, Ian became synonymous with relentless effort and spectacular goals. Whether it was a cheeky 30-yard chip or a clever toe-poke amidst a scramble in the box, Ian had an uncanny ability to score from anywhere.

1993 was a standout year as Ian helped Arsenal clinch a domestic cup Double, scoring crucial goals in the FA Cup and League Cup finals against Sheffield Wednesday. By the end of his Arsenal career, Ian had racked up an impressive 185 goals in 288 appearances. His induction into the Premier League Hall of Fame was a fitting tribute to a player who not only scored great goals but did so with a style and passion that exemplified the beautiful game. Thierry Henry, one of Arsenal's best players ever, said he fell in love with Arsenal because of Ian Wright.

PITCH TO PUNDIT

After hanging up his boots, Ian Wright didn't stray far from the world of football; instead, he swapped the grassy pitches for the glowing lights of the television studio, where he continued to inspire and entertain as only he can. With his iconic gold tooth gleaming and his earrings and diamond ring adding a dash of sparkle, Ian transitioned seamlessly into roles as a football pundit and presenter, carrying with him the same charisma that made him a favourite on the field.

Ian's approach to punditry is marked by his distinctive style — full of the rough language and 'tortured grammar' that makes him relatable. His straightforward, no-nonsense analysis cuts through the fluff, delivering insights with the sharpness of a well-practised striker. He combines a savvy understanding of the game with a street-smart wit, and openness that draws viewers in and keeps them engaged.

But Ian's role extends far beyond the camera's reach. In the community, he's affectionately known as "Uncle Ian," a nod to his approachable nature and his dedication to offering guidance and support, much like the cherished uncles who share life's crucial lessons. Ian understands the hurdles young players face, having navigated his fair share of challenges. Now, he's determined to give back, ensuring that aspiring footballers have the support they need to succeed.

His approach to mentoring is hands-on and heartfelt. Ian doesn't just teach techniques or tactics; he instils confidence and instigates a passion for the sport. Reflecting on how his mentor, Mr. Pigden, transformed his life by believing in him, Ian is driven to do the same for others. He works tirelessly to make football more inclusive, pushing for programmes that reach every corner of the community, allowing children from all backgrounds to play, learn, and grow.

LEGACY LIVES

Ian Wright's journey from the streets of South London to the heights of professional football is a tale brimming with lessons for young dreamers everywhere. It's a reminder that football isn't just about scoring goals or winning matches; it's about passion, resilience, and perseverance.

Imagine being told no time and again. Ian faced rejection after rejection when he tried out for football clubs, each one a door slamming shut. But did he give up? What Ian teaches us is that success isn't handed to us; we earn it through hard graft, resilience, and a never-say-die attitude. While talent is important, it's the heart you put into every match, every training session, and every moment on the field that truly counts.

Remember Ian's story whenever you feel like giving up. Whether it's in sports, studies, or any other passion you pursue, the path might not always be smooth, but it's your spirit, your grit, and your willingness to keep pushing forward that will define your success. Keep playing, keep learning, and never stop believing in yourself — because, like Ian, you could one day find yourself achieving more than you ever thought possible.

GARY LINEKER –
THE GENTLEMAN OF
FOOTBALL

"Respect your opponents, play fair, and always give your best effort. That's the true spirit of sportsmanship."

- Gary Lineker

PLAYING BY THE RULES

What makes Gary Lineker stand out isn't just the incredible goals he scored as a legendary striker, but also the remarkable fact that throughout his entire career, he never received a single yellow or red card. That's right, not one! Gary Lineker never once found himself in trouble with the referees.

Gary's journey to becoming a football legend began when he was just a kid, not much younger than you. Growing up in Leicester, England, football was his first love. From the moment he kicked his first football, he was hooked. He played every chance he got, whether in his backyard or at school, dreaming of one day playing professionally.

Starting at Leicester City, Gary had an incredible talent for scoring goals. His sharp football smarts and a gentle touch made each of his goals seem like a work of art. Being in just the right place at the right time, Gary made scoring goals look easy. He was like a football detective, always finding clues on the pitch that led him straight to the goal.

His skill took him to Everton, where he became the league's top scorer, then on to Barcelona, one of the most revered clubs in the world, where he helped the team win the Copa del Rey and the European Cup Winners' Cup. After his time in Barcelona, Gary returned to England to play for Tottenham Hotspur, where he continued to light up the Premier League with his goals. He won the FA Cup with Spurs, further adding to his list of achievements. But Gary Lineker will be remembered not just for the number of goals he scored but for how he played the game — with fairness and a joy that reminded everyone why they love football. His mastery on the club stage had prepared him for the grandest stage of them all – the World Cup.

GOLDEN BOOT GLORY

In the world of football, the 1986 World Cup holds a special place, and at the heart of this tournament's stories is one about an English player whose performance captured the imagination of fans everywhere. Gary, with his keen sense of the game, achieved something no other English player has managed to do, either before or since. He won the Golden Boot as the tournament's top scorer. Imagine scoring not one, not two, but six amazing goals in the biggest football tournament on the planet.

Gary's journey to becoming the top scorer started with a tough beginning. England struggled in their first two matches, but then came the game against Poland, which turned everything around. Gary scored a hat-trick – three goals in just one match! But Lineker didn't stop there – he continued his goal-scoring spree with two more goals against Paraguay, propelling England into the quarter-finals. Despite the challenges, Gary's brilliance was undeniable, adding another goal to his name in the quarter-final match against Argentina. Even though this match is often remembered for Maradona's controversial "Hand of God" goal, it was also a moment for Gary to shine once again.

FAIR PLAY AND SMILES

Gary's way of playing football was like a breath of fresh air. He believed in fair play, which means playing hard but playing clean. No tricks, no fouls, just pure skill and respect for everyone on the pitch. This wasn't always easy, especially in the heat of important matches, but Gary showed it was possible. His honesty on the pitch made him not just a favourite among his own fans but respected by opponents too.

In a world where sports figures are often idolised for their physical abilities, Gary Lineker stands out as a role model for his moral character and heart. In 1992, he was awarded an Order of the British Empire (OBE) for his services to football and his charitable work off the pitch. This wasn't just a medal to pin on his chest; it was a thank you from the whole country for being an amazing athlete and an even more amazing person. It was a recognition of his efforts to use his platform as a successful player to make a positive impact in the world. Whether it was helping children in need or supporting various charitable causes, Gary has always been at the forefront of making a difference.

After lighting up football pitches around the world, Gary Lineker didn't just hang up his boots and call it a day. Instead, he took his passion for the game to the next level by stepping into the world of journalism and sports broadcasting. Just like he dazzled fans with his goals on the pitch, Gary now dazzles viewers with his insights and charm on TV. He's become one of the most beloved television presenters and analysts, especially known for hosting "Match of the Day," a hugely popular football highlights and analysis.

But what really makes Gary's broadcasting career as memorable as his time on the pitch is his personality. Gary Lineker is famously witty and humorous, often showcasing his quick wit.

He has a knack for making viewers laugh while also making them think about the game in ways they hadn't before. Beyond just the laughs, Gary's broadcasting work is marked by a genuine respect for the game and its players. He's always fair in his analysis, bringing the same sportsmanship to journalism that he did to football.

A LESSON IN SPORTSMANSHIP

Gary showed that you can be competitive, strive to win, and still play by the rules, treating everyone with respect, whether you call it football or not. His attitude on the pitch teaches us that winning isn't everything if you lose your honour and respect for others along the way. He always played with a smile, showing that football, like all sports, should bring joy and friendship, not just trophies. Being a good sport is more important than the score at the end of the match.

Like Gary, we should aim to play our best, respect others, and keep our cool, even in the heat of the moment. We can all be champions in sports and in life, showing kindness, fairness, and a positive attitude no matter where we are or what we're doing. Remember, it's not just about how many goals you score, but how you play the game that truly counts.

SIR ALEX FERGUSON – TRIUMPH AND TEAMWORK

"The work of a team should always embrace a great player but the great player must always work."

- Alex Ferguson

THE MAKING OF A MASTERMIND

This story isn't a tale of a player who scored the winning goal or made the last-minute save; this is the story of Sir Alex Ferguson, a legendary football manager whose journey is a testament to belief and the magic of teamwork. Alex Ferguson wasn't just a manager; he was the architect of dreams, the mastermind behind one of the most successful eras in the history of Manchester United.

What truly set Alex Ferguson apart was his ability to inspire greatness. Like a conductor leading an orchestra, he knew how to bring out the best in everyone, creating harmony on the field that led to triumphs.

Born in the shadow of Glasgow's shipyards, Alex Ferguson knew that life was no easy game. The son of a shipbuilder, he learned early on that determination and grit were keys to overcoming obstacles. But Sir Alex's passion for football shone brighter than the brightest star in the Scottish sky. As years passed, his journey took him from the playing fields of Scotland to the managerial sidelines, where his vision, leadership, and relentless drive found their true purpose. But it was at Manchester United where Alex Ferguson would become a legend.

THE TREBLE TRIUMPH

The 1998-1999 season of Manchester United stands as a testament to what can be achieved when skill meets spirit. Embarking on a quest filled with challenges, they aimed to capture not one, not two, but three of the most coveted trophies in football.

As the season kicked off, Manchester United had their eyes set on the stars. Their journey through the Premier League was like a roller coaster ride, filled with breathtaking highs and nail-biting lows. Yet, through every challenge, the team's spirit never wavered. Their passion and grit on the field propelled them forward, match after match, until they were crowned the champions of England.

But their quest for glory didn't stop there. The FA Cup awaited, a trophy steeped in history and prestige. Game after game, Manchester United battled their way through the competition, showcasing their skill, unity, and an unbreakable will to win. They lifted the trophy high, marking their second major triumph of the season.

However, it was in the Champions League where the true magic happened, where a story so dramatic unfolded that it would forever be remembered as the "Miracle of Camp Nou." On a starry night in Barcelona, Manchester United faced Bayern Munich, a formidable opponent. As the game progressed, it seemed as though the dream of the treble was slipping away. With Bayern leading by one goal and the clock ticking down, hope was thinning. But Manchester United was not a team to give up easily. With just seconds left on the clock, Manchester United scored not one, but two incredible goals. The stadium erupted in disbelief and joy as Manchester United turned defeat into victory, clinching the Champions League title and completing their historic treble.

The team's dramatic comeback in the final was a testament to their resilience, belief, and the magic that happens when you never stop fighting. The goals in injury time weren't just shots into the net; they were messages of hope, symbols of what can be achieved when you refuse to give up, no matter how dark the moment may seem.

After leading Manchester United to an unbelievable season, Alex Ferguson received one of the highest honours not just in football, but in the entire world. Queen Elizabeth II knighted him, transforming him from Alex Ferguson to Sir Alex Ferguson, a knight of the realm!

BUILDING DYNASTIES ON THE PITCH

At the heart of Sir Alex's legacy is his nurturing of The Class of '92, a group of young talents including David Beckham, Nicky Butt, Ryan Giggs, Paul Scholes, and the Neville brothers, Gary and Phil. Like a skilled gardener tending to his plants, Ferguson cultivated these players' talents, blending them with the strength and wisdom of experienced team members. He understood that to build a dominant team, he needed more than just physical skill; he needed to foster a spirit of unity, a deep-seated belief in teamwork.

But Sir Alex's brilliance wasn't just in recognizing talent; it was in his ability to adapt, to continuously rebuild teams that could stand the test of time and competition. As the years rolled on, he seamlessly integrated new players into the squad, ensuring that United's winning culture remained intact. His vision was clear: to maintain a team not just for a season, but for generations, always staying one step ahead, always evolving - he built eras. A testament to this was the 2007 season, a decade after their iconic treble win, when Manchester United secured the domestic titles and once again clinched the Champions League title.

THE POWER OF TEAMWORK

One of the most magical moments that encapsulate Ferguson's mastery in nurturing teamwork and camaraderie happened in the 2008 Champions League final in Moscow. Before the match, as tension filled the air, Ferguson gathered his warriors for what would become one of the most inspiring speeches in football history. The dressing room fell silent, the air thick with anticipation, as Ferguson began to speak. "I've already won," he declared, leaving his players puzzled. "This is my victory," Ferguson exclaimed. But it wasn't about the score or the battle against Chelsea; Ferguson was speaking of a deeper victory, one that transcended trophies and titles. It was a masterstroke of motivation, weaving the players' individual stories into the fabric of the team's identity. He took the time to acknowledge each player's journey, from Evra's path to Manchester, Rooney's fiery spirit, to Park Ji-sung's resilience. In that room, they were no longer just athletes from different parts of the world; they were brothers, fighting for a common cause. It was about the fellowship they had forged, the brotherhood they had become. They were a family, united by their love for the game and their commitment to each other.

The match itself was a rollercoaster, a clash of titans that pushed both teams to their limits. Yet, in the end, it was Manchester United who emerged victorious, their spirit of unity shining brighter than the Moscow night.

TOGETHER TO THE TOP

Ferguson's leadership was about more than just tactics or discipline; it was about instilling a sense of belonging, of shared purpose among his players. He knew that to achieve greatness, they needed to believe in each other, to support one another through every challenge and every triumph. He fostered an environment where players felt valued, understood, and connected.

His ability to bring out the best in them, not just as players but as individuals, was central to Manchester United's success.

So, to all the young dreamers out there, remember: football is more than a game. It's a lesson in unity, a celebration of teamwork, and a journey that teaches us that together, nothing is impossible. Let Ferguson's Reds inspire you to chase your dreams, support your teammates, and believe in the power of "us."

LUIS SUAREZ – REDEMPTION ROAD

"The best thing is to look ahead and not behind"

- Luis Suarez

GOALS, GRIT, AND CONTROVERSIES

Luis Suarez is a name that lights up the world of football with his incredible skills and unforgettable moments on the pitch. Growing up in Salto, Uruguay, Luis always had a football at his feet, dreaming of playing professionally. His journey wasn't easy; he faced many challenges, including moving away from his family at a young age to join a youth football academy in Montevideo. He quickly rose through the ranks, showcasing his knack for scoring goals and his fierce competitiveness on the pitch, and it wasn't long before his amazing ability to score goals caught the attention of big clubs in Europe.

However, Suarez's career has also been marked by some controversies that have sparked a lot of discussions. From on-pitch incidents to moments of intense competition, Luis's journey has had its share of ups and downs. But these stories, which we'll explore later, are part of what makes his career so interesting. These moments remind us that even the greatest talents can face challenges and make mistakes. But Suarez's career also shows that it's possible to learn from those mistakes, work hard to improve, and continue to pursue your dreams with passion and dedication.

THE ART OF GOAL SCORING

Luis Suarez, with his unparalleled goal-scoring ability and agility, has mesmerised football fans around the world. His style of play is a blend of passion and precision, making him one of the most exciting forwards to watch. His ability to anticipate where the ball will be and position himself accordingly has led to some of the most memorable goals in football history.

Beyond his technical skills, Suarez's playing style is marked by his intensity and passion. Whether he's chasing down a ball or celebrating a goal, his emotions are always on full display, embodying the heart and soul he puts into every match.

Throughout his career, Suarez has achieved remarkable success with clubs across Europe. At Ajax, he became a scoring sensation, helping the team clinch the Eredivisie title. His move to Liverpool saw Suarez elevate his game even further, earning him the PFA Players' Player of the Year and the European Golden Shoe awards. With Liverpool, he set a record for the most goals in a single Premier League season, leaving fans in awe of his talent. However, it was with Barcelona that Suarez truly cemented his legacy, winning numerous titles and another European Golden Shoe. He broke records, becoming Barcelona's all-time leading scorer in a single La Liga season, showcasing his extraordinary ability to find the back of the net.

However, his achievements are not limited to club success; Suarez has also shone brightly on the international stage. Representing Uruguay in multiple World Cups, he has displayed his talent against the best in the world, scoring crucial goals and helping his country reach the semi-finals.

THE SAVE THAT SHOOK THE WORLD

In one of the most unforgettable moments of football history, Luis Suarez found himself at the centre of a huge debate during the 2010 World Cup match between Uruguay and Ghana. With just seconds left in extra time, and the score tied, Ghana had a chance to win with a powerful shot heading straight for the goal. Suarez, standing on the goal line, did something unexpected: he used his hands to block the ball, preventing what seemed like a certain goal. This act got him a red card – he was sent off the pitch – and Ghana was awarded a penalty kick. However, Ghana missed the penalty, and Uruguay went on to win the match in a penalty shootout.

This incident sparked a big debate: Was Suarez's action cheating, or was it a sacrifice for his team? Some people say Suarez cheated because using your hands is against the rules unless you're the goalkeeper, which he wasn't. Others argue that Suarez did what he felt was necessary to help his team, knowing well that he would face consequences, like being sent off and missing the next game. This moment in football history is a reminder that sports can present difficult moral decisions, and what matters most is how we face the consequences of our actions.

A TEST OF TEMPERAMENT

On three different occasions, Suarez found himself in the spotlight for something quite unusual on the football pitch: he bit an opponent.

One of the most talked-about incidents happened during a high-stakes World Cup game in 2014, Uruguay vs. Italy. This action, more suited to a dramatic film than a football match, unfolded in seconds but will be remembered for a lifetime. In a moment charged with tension, Suarez, driven by an intense desire to win, bit the Italian defender, leaving everyone watching in shock.

The consequences of Suarez's action were swift and severe. Football's governing body handed down a lengthy suspension, sidelining him for many crucial matches and sparking debates around the globe. This wasn't the first time Suarez had faced such a penalty for biting; it was his third, making the repercussions even more significant. Each suspension served as a stark reminder of the importance of self-control and the high standards of behaviour expected from professional athletes.

You might wonder, why would such a talented player do something like this? It's hard to say for sure. Perhaps it's a momentary lapse in judgement, or maybe the immense pressure and intensity of the game can lead players to act out of character. Whatever the reason, these moments remind us that even our heroes face challenges in managing their emotions and actions under pressure.

TURNING THE PAGE

After facing challenges, including moments that surprised everyone, Suarez didn't let them define his career. Instead, he looked at them as opportunities to grow and learn. It's like when you're playing a video game and you keep getting stuck at the same tough level. Instead of giving up, you try to learn from each mistake, getting a little better each time. That's what Suarez did; he expressed regret, sought help to improve his behaviour, and focused even more on being the best player he could be. Through hard work and a heartfelt desire to be better, he began his journey to redemption. He showed the world his true character, not just as a top football player but as someone willing to make positive changes.

This commitment to betterment paved the way for a new chapter with Inter Miami in 2023 where Suarez embraced the opportunity to not only demonstrate his undiminished skills on the pitch but also to lead by example, showing young teammates that growth and improvement are always possible, no matter the past.

FROM ADVERSITY TO REDEMPTION

Sometimes, in the heat of the moment, Luis let his emotions get the better of him, leading to decisions that he would later regret. These incidents remind us all about the importance of staying calm, respecting others, and playing fair. It shows that losing control not only affects us but also our team and the people around us. Understanding how to manage our feelings, especially when things get tough, is a crucial skill, not just in sports but in life.

Like a hero in an epic tale, Suarez faced significant adversity, moments that tested his character and could have sidelined his story. But instead of letting these challenges defeat him, he saw them as obstacles that were meant to be overcome. He recognised his mistakes and took responsibility for them showing us the power of second chances and the strength it takes to change. Suarez's journey teaches us that true greatness on the pitch comes not only from skill but also from the strength of character, from how we handle our lowest moments and how we strive to be better every day. While everyone makes mistakes, it's how we respond to them that truly defines us.

JAVIER 'CHICHARITO' HERNANDEZ – RADIATING POSITIVITY

"I always give my best, because that's what I have control over."

- Javier 'Chicharito' Hernandez

Once upon a time, in the bustling streets of Guadalajara, Mexico, there was a young boy named Javier Hernández who loved nothing more than to play football. This boy would one day become known to the world as Chicharito, meaning "little pea." This unique nickname was lovingly given by his father, Javier Hernández Sr., who was also a professional footballer known as "Chícharo" or "pea" because of his green eyes.

Chicharito's journey was not a sprint but a marathon, paved with challenges that tested his mettle at every turn. His big break came when he donned the colours of Chivas Guadalajara, a team that would be the launchpad for his ascent to stardom. Here, he honed his craft, becoming a goal-scoring sensation, celebrated for his lightning-fast reflexes and an uncanny ability to be at the right place, at the right time, turning the tide of matches with the flick of his boot.

But it was his move to Manchester United that catapulted him into the global spotlight. Chicharito became known as the "super-sub," a player who might not always start the match but could always be counted on to make a difference when he came off the bench. His knack for scoring crucial goals in the dying minutes of a match won his team points and stole the hearts of fans.

But what made Chicharito a hero wasn't just his ability to score goals; it was how he played the game. With a smile that could light up the darkest of nights and a joy that was contagious, he reminded us all that at its heart, football is a celebration of skill, teamwork, and the sheer love of the game.

THE ROUND TRIP

After leaving the bright lights of Manchester, Chicharito's football journey continued to unfold with twists and turns that took him across Europe and eventually back to the shores of America before a heartfelt return to where it all began.

His next destination was the sunny lands of Spain, where he joined Real Madrid. He might not have been the biggest star of Galácticos, but he shone brightly, especially when he scored a decisive goal against Atlético in the Champions League. That moment was pure magic, showing his ability to be the hero when his team needed him the most.

The adventure didn't stop there. Chicharito then made a bold move to Germany, signing with Bayer Leverkusen. In the Bundesliga, his skills flourished like never before. He was a goal machine, breaking records and becoming the first Mexican player to score in five consecutive Bundesliga matches. In Germany, he wasn't just a "super-sub"; he was a superstar, beloved by fans for his joyous celebrations and humble personality.

The call of the Premier League beckoned once more, and Chicharito answered, joining West

Ham United. Back in England, he continued to showcase his talents, scoring on his debut and reminding fans of his predatory instincts in front of goal. Though his time with the Hammers had its ups and downs, Chicharito's work ethic and positive attitude never wavered.

Then came a new chapter in Chicharito's career, one that would take him across the Atlantic to the LA Galaxy in Major League Soccer. At the Galaxy, he worked tirelessly, connecting with fans in Los Angeles and beyond, proving that his love for football knows no boundaries.

But every story has its homecoming, and for Chicharito, that meant a return to where it all began: Guadalajara. Returning to Chivas was more than just another signing; it was a hero's return. The club where he first dreamed of football stardom welcomed him back with open arms. Back in the familiar red and white stripes, Chicharito was living his dream once again, in front of the fans who saw him grow from a young hopeful into a global football icon.

Chicharito has encountered hurdles that tested his spirit, too. Yet, through every challenge, he carried a secret weapon stronger than any defender's tackle: his unbreakable positivity and optimism.

Picture this: a crucial match is underway, the crowd is roaring, and the pressure is as thick as a goal net. But our hero finds himself on the bench, sidelined during moments when his heart aches to be on the field, racing towards the goal. For many, this would be a storm cloud over their passion, but for Chicharito, it was just another challenge to overcome. When he was not selected to play, instead of letting frustration affect his vision, he chose to see it as a chance to learn, to cheer for his teammates, and to prepare for his next opportunity. His belief was as solid as a football, round and complete; he knew his time to shine would come again. He understood that football, like life, is full of ups and downs, and that the true victory lies in staying positive and never giving up.

His infectious positivity wasn't just for himself; it spread like wildfire among his teammates, coaches, and fans. In moments when the team's spirit was low, when the scoreboard wasn't in their favour, or when the path to victory seemed clouded, Chicharito's unwavering belief and smile became the team's armour. He reminded everyone that joy and optimism are powers mighty enough to turn the tide of any battle.

This attitude didn't go unnoticed. Fans around the world were drawn to Chicharito not just for his skill on the field but for his ability to remain hopeful and joyful, no matter the circumstances. His positivity became his signature, as recognisable as his name on the back of his jersey. Young fans learned from him that no matter what challenges lie ahead, whether in football, school, or life's many adventures, facing them with a smile and a positive attitude can make all the difference.

Through every high and low of his career, Chicharito's optimism was the thread that tied his story together. It was there in his first goal for a new club, echoing in his celebrations. It was there in every setback, whispering that tomorrow would bring another chance. And it was there in his triumphant return to the field, brighter and more determined than ever.

Off the pitch, Chicharito's uplifting attitude shines just as brightly. He greets fans with a warmth that melts hearts, signs autographs with a smile that lights up his face, and speaks with a sincerity that speaks volumes of his character. He understands the power of a kind word, a simple gesture, and he gives these gifts freely, uplifting those around him and spreading a message of hope and positivity.

THE BRIGHT SIDE OF THE GAME

Chicharito's impact on football is immeasurable, not just in the goals he scores, but in the hearts he touches. Through every moment spent watching from the sidelines, every challenge, his optimism never dimmed. It was his shield against doubt, his light in the darkness, guiding him back onto the field with renewed vigour and passion. Chicharito's story is a testament to the power of a positive spirit, showing us that while we may not always control the game, we can always control how we play it in our hearts.

But remember, being optimistic doesn't mean ignoring the reality of a situation. It means facing it head-on, with the belief that you have what it takes to overcome it. It's about being the light for your teammates, friends, and family, showing them that even on the cloudiest days, the sun can shine through.

Just like Chicharito, we can all be champions of our own stories, with positivity as our guiding star. We can choose to face each day with optimism and to see every challenge as an opportunity to grow stronger and more resilient. So, let's wear our smiles as proudly as our jerseys, and remember that no matter what happens, our spirits can never be benched.

VINICIUS JR – STANDING STRONG AGAINST RACISM

"Our differences make us stronger. Embracing them makes us champions"

- Vinicius Jr.

RISING STAR

Vinicius Jr., the dazzling winger for Real Madrid, is swiftly becoming one of football's brightest stars. His journey from the lively streets of Rio de Janeiro to the iconic Santiago Bernabéu Stadium is a tale of extraordinary talent and determination. But beyond his spectacular goals and electrifying runs down the pitch, Vini Jr. stands out for his courageous stand against racism, using his platform to promote equality and respect in football.

Born in the football-crazy city of Rio, Vinicius started kicking a ball almost as soon as he could walk. He grew up idolising Brazilian legends like Ronaldo and Ronaldinho, dreaming of one day echoing their wizardry on the field. His talent was evident early on, and by the age of 10, he was already turning heads at Flamengo, one of Brazil's top football clubs.

Vinicius's major breakthrough came at just 16. His performances in Brazil's youth leagues were nothing short of sensational, earning him a place in Flamengo's senior team. It wasn't long before Europe's top clubs were competing for his signature. Real Madrid, one of the world's most prestigious clubs, soon signed him, and at the tender age of 18, Vinicius made the bold move to Spain, ready to prove himself on one of the grandest stages in football.

Vinicius's early appearances were promising, marked by a debut in which he came on as a late substitute in a tense match against Atlético Madrid. He quickly became a regular first-team player, known for his crucial goals. His profound impact was highlighted when he scored the winning goal in the 2022 Champions League final against Liverpool, securing Madrid's 14th title in the competition. His contributions to the club were further recognised when he inherited the iconic No. 7 shirt, underscoring his importance to the team and his status among the elite players.

However, Vinicius's rise to stardom in Europe wasn't without its obstacles. As a young, prominent Black athlete, he encountered racism, both on and off the pitch. This ugly side of the sport showed itself through hurtful chants and comments, attempting to diminish his achievements and resolve. But Vinicius refused to let these incidents sideline him. Instead, they fuelled his determination to excel and use his growing influence to fight against racism, showing courage that far exceeded his years.

A SPARK IGNITES

One notable incident occurred during a heated match against Valencia, where Vinicius was subjected to hurtful chants from the stands. The young star's reaction was both dignified and inspiring. Instead of retaliating or letting the negativity affect his game, Vinicius responded on the pitch by playing even harder, demonstrating that excellence and integrity can drown out hate.

The reaction from the public and the football community was immediate and supportive. Fans around the world rallied on social media, condemning the racism and expressing solidarity with Vinicius. His teammates at Real Madrid and players from other clubs also stood by him, demonstrating that in the world of football, there is no room for racism. Icons of the sport and even rivals took to various platforms to support Vinicius, sending a powerful message against discrimination.

Personally, these experiences deeply impacted Vinicius. Initially, they were disheartening, challenging his love for the game and shaking his spirits. However, Vinicius chose to channel these trials into a force for positive change. He became more vocal about the issue of racism in football, using his platform to advocate for a more inclusive and respectful sports environment. His message was clear: racism has no place in football or any other part of society.

Professionally, the challenges spurred Vinicius to greater heights. Each incident sharpened his focus and determination, pushing him to perform better and prove his detractors wrong.

His response on the pitch spoke volumes—instead of succumbing to the pressure, he excelled, scoring crucial goals and helping his team clinch victories in critical matches. His ability to rise above adversity not only won him games but also earned him the respect and admiration of fans, teammates, and even opponents.

A HERO FOR TODAY

Vinicius's stand against racism resonated around the globe, earning him a legion of supporters. In a stunning display of solidarity, the famous Christ the Redeemer statue in Brazil went dark one evening, symbolising the world standing with Vinicius in the dark times of battling racism. Back in his home state, lawmakers passed the "Vini. Jr. law," a groundbreaking initiative aimed at fighting racist behaviour in sports.

Stepping onto an even bigger stage, Vinicius was chosen by FIFA to lead a new anti-racism task force. This group, made up of players from across the globe, is set to propose tougher penalties for those displaying racist behaviour in football. It's a big responsibility, showing that the world trusts Vinicius not just to score goals but to help lead the way in creating a fairer, more respectful sporting world.

For his bravery and dedication, Vinicius was honoured in various ways back in Brazil. He received prestigious awards from legislative bodies, and his footprints were even added to a famous walk of fame, right alongside football greats like Pelé and Ronaldo. These honours are not just for his football skills but for his strength of character.

On the field, Vinicius continues to fight racism by participating in special matches organised to raise awareness. He played in friendlies against Guinea and Senegal, and there are plans for a high-profile game against Spain at Real Madrid's own stadium, the Bernabeu, all part of a broader anti-racism campaign. These aren't just games; they're powerful statements that football stands united against racism.

Off the field, Vinicius is making a difference through the Instituto Vini Jr., an initiative he started to combat social inequality in Brazil. The institute focuses on education, providing young people with the tools they need to succeed in today's digital world. For his efforts, Vinicius received the Socrates Award, which honours footballers who are deeply committed to making a social impact.

THE POWER OF SPEAKING UP

Imagine you're in the middle of an exciting football match. The crowd is cheering, the game is intense, and then someone says something unkind about another player's background. What would you do? For young sports enthusiasts, this is where the lesson begins. It's about being brave enough to say, "That's not right" and showing others that respect is part of the game, both on and off the field.

Football, like many other sports, reflects society, and sometimes it mirrors the parts we are not proud of. The battle against racism in football is tough, but with players like Vinicius Jr. leading the charge, there's hope. Every time he addresses racism, whether through a tweet, an interview, or his involvement in anti-racism campaigns, he's scoring a goal for justice.

Vini Jr. teaches us that when someone tries to hurt others with words or actions, standing up and speaking out can stop it from happening again. He shows that being a great player isn't just about skill and tactics — it's also about character and courage. Vinicius Jr. uses his fame to speak against racism, showing us that our voices are powerful, even if we feel small.

Every time you play, whether it's a friendly kickabout in the park or a school tournament, you have a chance to make a difference. How you treat your teammates and opponents can change the game. If you learn to stand up for what's right from the start, there's no telling how far you'll go, both in sports and in life. Remember: in the big match against racism, we're all on the same team. Let's play fair, let's play bold, and let's play together. Because that's how we all win — by respecting each other on and off the pitch.

ZLATAN IBRAHIMOVIC – UNWAVERING CONFIDENCE

"I am Zlatan Ibrahimovic, who are you?"

\- Zlatan Ibrahimovic

A PERSONALITY AS BOLD AS HIS GAME

Zlatan Ibrahimovic's story begins in the city of Malmö, Sweden, where he grew up in a working-class neighbourhood known as Rosengård. Imagine streets lined with rows of simple houses, playgrounds echoing with the laughter and shouts of children, and a community where every family works hard to make ends meet. This was Zlatan's world, a place full of life but also challenges. As an immigrant child, Zlatan often felt like an outsider, struggling to find his place in a society that seemed worlds apart from his family's origins in the Balkans. The cold Swedish winters and long, dark nights could make Rosengård feel even more isolating for a young boy with dreams bigger than his surroundings.

But amidst these challenges, Zlatan found a friend in football. The local football fields became his sanctuary, a place where he could run free, away from the difficulties of daily life. With every dribble, every goal, Zlatan wasn't just playing; he was speaking in a language everyone could understand — excellence on the pitch. Football gave him a voice, a way to express his frustrations, ambitions, and joy. It was on these humble fields that Zlatan's extraordinary talent began to shine, offering him a glimpse of a life beyond Rosengård, a life filled with possibilities.

When Zlatan Ibrahimovic was just starting out in football, he didn't play like everyone else. Imagine mixing high-flying martial arts moves with football; that's what Zlatan did! Thanks to his training in taekwondo, he could do things on the pitch that amazed everyone. He could jump higher, kick harder, and move in ways that other players couldn't even dream of. His unique style made football more than just a game; it was a show, with Zlatan as the star performer.

But being different isn't always easy. Zlatan's confidence and way of speaking his mind made coaches and critics unsure about him. Instead of being quiet and fitting in, Zlatan was bold and spoke his truth, which sometimes made waves. Yet, he saw his personality as a strength, not something to hide. He believed in himself, even when others doubted him. This belief wasn't just talk; it pushed him to work harder, to practise more, and to turn those doubts into fuel for his fire.

STRIKING THROUGH EUROPE

Zlatan Ibrahimovic's football journey soared to new heights when he signed with Ajax, the renowned Dutch club celebrated for nurturing young talent into global football stars. It was at Ajax that Zlatan began carving out his legacy, clinching two Eredivisie titles and a KNVB Cup, showcasing his innate knack for scoring and his destined path to football greatness.

The adventure didn't end in the Netherlands for Zlatan; it was just the beginning. He then took his talents to Juventus in Italy, a country where football isn't just a sport, but a way of life. At Juventus, despite facing stiff competition and high expectations, Zlatan's unique blend of skill and determination saw him rise above challenges. He contributed significantly to the team, making an indelible mark and helping Juventus secure two Serie A titles. The saga continued as he transferred to Inter Milan, further cementing his status as a top-tier striker. At Inter, Zlatan was instrumental in securing three consecutive Serie A titles, leaving an indelible mark with his scoring prowess.

Zlatan's relentless pursuit of success led him to another iconic Italian club, AC Milan, where his influence was immediate. With Milan, he clinched another Serie A title, adding to his impressive collection of trophies and reiterating his ability to make a significant impact at any club. His remarkable achievements laid the groundwork for the next chapter of his storied career, leading to a much-anticipated move to Barcelona.

FROM BARCELONA TO BEYOND

When Zlatan joined Barcelona, one of the most famous football clubs in the world, it was like a dream come true. Barcelona was a team known for playing some of the most beautiful football, and now Zlatan was going to be a part of it. During his time at Barcelona, Zlatan added more trophies to his collection, including the Spanish League title and the Super Cup. He scored some spectacular goals, showing off his incredible talent on an even bigger stage.

However, even in a team filled with stars, relationships matter a lot, and Zlatan's time at Barcelona had its ups and downs, especially with the coach, Pep Guardiola. They had different ideas about football and how Zlatan should play, which sometimes made things challenging. This situation raises an interesting question: in a football team, who's more important – the star player or the manager? Is it the manager's strategy and guidance that leads a team to victory, or is it the star player's skill and determination on the field?

Imagine being at the top of your game but feeling like you're not fitting in with the team's plans. That's how Zlatan felt. But instead of letting this get him down, Zlatan's strong belief in himself guided his next steps. He knew he had more to offer, more goals to score, and more trophies to win. This self-belief is what makes Zlatan stand out. Zlatan Ibrahimovic decided to leave Barcelona, and his adventure led him to Paris Saint-Germain (PSG), where he truly shone. At PSG, Zlatan wasn't just a player; he became a superstar. He scored goals almost as if by magic, leading PSG to win four league titles in a row! Zlatan showed everyone that no matter where he played, he could help his team win, becoming a legend in Paris with his incredible talent and unforgettable moments on the pitch.

Zlatan's adventure didn't stop in Europe. He decided to move to the United States to play for LA Galaxy. He believed in himself so much that he took out a full-page newspaper ad simply saying, "You're welcome." This showed not just his confidence but also his unique way of

introducing himself to football fans in the U.S.
He was sure he would make a huge impact.

ZLATAN'S WAY

Zlatan Ibrahimovic is not just any football
player; he's like a superhero from the pages of a
comic book, with a larger-than-life personality
and the kind of self-belief that makes you think
he can do just about anything on the football
pitch. Zlatan doesn't just hope he's going to
score; he believes in his ability to make the
impossible possible, turning football matches
into his own personal highlight reel. Zlatan
knows he's different, and he wouldn't have it
any other way.

Even when critics doubted him or suggested he
change his style of play to fit in better, Zlatan
refused to be anyone but himself. He knows that
his unique approach to football, combining
creativity, strength, and skill, is what makes him
special. Zlatan plays by his own rules, refusing
to change his style or quiet his personality to fit
anyone else's expectations. Whether it's taking

bold shots that others wouldn't dare attempt or speaking his mind in interviews, Zlatan stays true to himself.

MASTERING THE ART OF SELF BELIEF

Zlatan's journey teaches us a valuable lesson: believing in yourself and your abilities is powerful. He shows us that it's okay to stand out, to be different, and to have confidence in what makes you unique. In a world that often tells us to conform, Zlatan inspires us to stand tall and be proud of who we are and what we can achieve.

Embrace your individuality and believe in your abilities, even when it feels like everybody is doubting you. Don't let criticism deter you from pursuing your dreams. Instead, like Zlatan, use it to push yourself further. Remember, the only person who needs to believe in your dreams is you. By staying true to yourself and working hard, you can achieve anything you set your mind   to.

NEYMAR JR –
THE JOYFUL JOURNEY

"I play with joy and passion, and that's why I love the game of football."

- Neymar Jr.

THE DANCE OF FOOTBALL

In the vibrant heart of Brazil, where football beats like a rhythmic drum across the streets and beaches, a young boy with boundless energy and dreams as big as the sky was beginning his journey. This isn't just any story; it's the tale of Neymar Jr., who has danced his way into the history books as one of football's most electrifying talents.

Imagine a young boy in Mogi das Cruzes, Brazil, where the love for football runs as deep as the Amazon River. This boy, Neymar, didn't have fancy footballs or shoes. Instead, he played barefoot in the streets, using makeshift balls crafted from socks or anything he could find. But what he lacked in equipment, he made up for with a boundless passion for the game and a dream that one day he'd play among the stars.

Despite not having much, Neymar's family shared a rich love for football, a bond that fuelled his early love for the game. His father, a former football player, saw the spark in

Neymar's eyes and knew his son had something special. Soon, the young prodigy found himself at Santos FC, where he began to turn his dreams into reality. Neymar wasn't just playing; he was performing, dancing with the ball in a way that captivated anyone who watched. His skills were about bringing joy, a celebration, influenced by Brazil's rhythm and style, known as "*joga bonito*" – the beautiful play.

From Santos to Barcelona, and then to Paris Saint-Germain, Neymar's career has been a thrilling ride, filled with jaw-dropping goals, dazzling assists, and moments of pure brilliance. Yet, through all the fame and accolades, he remains the boy from Mogi das Cruzes, playing the game he loves with the joy of a child and the heart of a champion.

THE BEAUTIFUL GAME

Joga Bonito. This phrase captures the essence of Brazilian magic on the pitch; it's a celebration of creativity, flair, and passion for the game. And among its greatest modern exponents is

Neymar, a player whose skills on the pitch are as mesmerising as a carnival in Rio. He embodies Joga Bonito like no other, carrying on the legacy of Brazilian greats like Pelé, Zico, Romário, and Ronaldinho – a legacy of playing with joy, no matter the pressure or the stakes.

Neymar's ability to smile, to dance after a goal, to play with the freedom of a child in the streets, brings a lightness to the game that's both refreshing and inspiring. Neymar brings a sense of wonder to the pitch, a reminder that at its heart, football is about expressing oneself freely and embracing one's talents.

OVERCOMING CHALLENGES WITH A SMILE

Neymar carries a story that's as much about soaring triumphs as it is about overcoming obstacles. Triumphs, oh, they have been many. Neymar's trophy cabinet sparkles with accolades – from domestic league titles in Spain and France to the coveted Champions League trophy. But he has faced his fair share of challenges, too.

Injuries have been a recurring villain in Neymar's tale. One of the most heart-wrenching moments came during the 2014 World Cup, held in his homeland. Neymar, carrying the hopes of a nation, was struck down by a severe back injury in the quarter-finals. It was a moment that could have dimmed the brightest of stars, but not Neymar. His resilience shone through. With determination and a relentless spirit, he bounced back, showing the world that a true champion never gives up.

Criticism also has been a constant companion on Neymar's journey. Whether it was about his playing style, or about his moves off the pitch, Neymar faced it all. But instead of letting the critics get to him, he used their words as fuel. Neymar's response was always on the field – showing the world his skill, and an undying passion for football.

DRIBBLING TOWARDS A BETTER FUTURE

Imagine a place where children's laughter fills the air, where the joy of learning and playing football brings smiles to faces that have seen hardship and struggle. This place is real, thanks to Neymar's big dream. He founded the Instituto Projeto Neymar Jr., a magical fortress not of bricks and mortar, but of hope and dreams for thousands of kids in Brazil. Here, Neymar's vision comes to life, offering education, sports, and health care to children, ensuring their future is as bright as a stadium floodlight. Neymar shows us that the real victory is in helping others score goals in life.

Neymar's heart beats not just for football but also for the world. He steps up to the plate, ready to tackle global issues head-on. Whether it's raising awareness for critical diseases, supporting disaster relief efforts, or standing up for children's rights, Neymar plays a pivotal role. His philanthropic efforts are like a perfect pass in a crucial match, setting up opportunities for change and improvement in the lives of many.

But Neymar's influence stretches even further, diving into the colourful world of popular culture. Through social media, Neymar shares snapshots of his life, victories, and challenges, reminding everyone that heroes have their battles too. He encourages his followers to stay positive, to work hard, and to never stop dreaming.

FINDING JOY IN EVERY KICK

Neymar's journey reminds us that no matter where you come from, your dreams are valid. He still plays with the same joy and passion that lit up those early games on the streets of Brazil. Football, much like life, is not just about the score at the end but about how beautifully you played, how freely you expressed yourself, and how much joy you found along the way. Neymar shows us that to truly excel, to truly shine, we must be brave enough to embrace our creativity. This is the heart of "Joga Bonito," where the game becomes a dance, and each player, a dancer, moving to the rhythm of their heart.

So, the next time you find yourself on the field of life, facing challenges or chasing dreams, remember to play beautifully, live joyfully, and shine brightly, just like the stars in the night sky, reminding us all that the most beautiful goals are those scored with a smile.

CONCLUSION

As we reach the final whistle of "Amazing Football Stories for Kids," we've journeyed together across pitches far and wide, from bustling cities to quiet towns, learning about the legends who have made football the beautiful game it is today. These stories, filled with breathtaking goals and heartwarming moments of sportsmanship, remind us that football is more than just a game — it's a universal language that brings people together, celebrating our differences and uniting us in our love for the game.

The legends we've met in these pages — each with their own unique story — share common virtues that have propelled them to greatness. Perseverance, facing each challenge head-on, never giving up no matter how tough the match gets. Determination, pushing themselves to be better every day, on and off the pitch. And passion, that burning love for the game that drives them to achieve the extraordinary.

These values are not just for football legends; they are for you, too. Whether you're on the pitch scoring goals, in the classroom solving problems, or at home helping your family, these principles can guide you. Pursue your passions with the dedication and positive attitude of your football heroes. Embrace hard work, discipline, and self-belief. Remember, every legend started with a dream, facing obstacles and doubters, but through resilience and tireless effort, they turned their dreams into reality.

So, as we close this book, let the stories of these football legends inspire you to dream big. Football is more than just winning or losing; it's about the journey, the friends you make along the way, and the lessons you learn. Remember, the next chapter of football history is waiting to be written, and it could be by you. With every kick, pass, and goal, you're not just playing a game; you're carrying forward the legacy of those who came before you, adding your own story to the rich tapestry of football.

Printed in Great Britain
by Amazon